Creative Crafts for Kids

Friendship CRAFTS

By Helen Skillicorn

Gareth Stevens
Publishing

Please visit our Web site www.garethstevens.com. For a free color catalog of all our high-quality books, call toll free 1-800-542-2595 or fax 1-877-542-2596.

Library of Congress Cataloging-in-Publication Data
Skillicorn, Helen.
   Friendship crafts / Helen Skillicorn.
      p. cm. — (Creative crafts for kids)
   Includes index.
   ISBN 978-1-4339-3558-9 (library binding)
   ISBN 978-1-4339-3559-6 (pbk.)
   ISBN 978-1-4339-3560-2 (6-pack)
   1. Handicraft—Juvenile literature. I. Title.
TT157.S5324 2010
745.5—dc22   2009041571

Published in 2010 by
Gareth Stevens Publishing
111 East 14th Street, Suite 349
New York, NY 10003

© 2010 The Brown Reference Group Ltd.

For Gareth Stevens Publishing:
Art Direction: Haley Harasymiw
Editorial Direction: Kerri O'Donnell

For The Brown Reference Group Ltd:
Editorial Director: Lindsey Lowe
Managing Editor: Tim Harris
Children's Publisher: Anne O'Daly
Design Manager: David Poole
Production Director: Alastair Gourlay

Picture Credits:
All photographs: Martin Norris
Front Cover: Corbis: Richard T. Nowitz and Martin Norris

Manufactured in the United States of America
1 2 3 4 5 6 7 8 9   12 11 10

CPSIA compliance information: Batch #BRW0102GS: For further information contact Gareth Stevens, New York, New York at 1-800-542-2595.

Contents

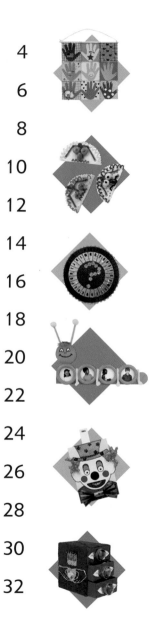

Introduction

Friendship Crafts is filled with ideas for special things to make for special friends. Make the smile card on page 24 as a cheer-up gift or the pirate portrait on page 22 for you and all your friends to have fun with—each can peer through the picture and get a photo taken as a grizzly pirate.

YOU WILL NEED

Each project includes a list of all the things you need.

Before you go out and buy lots of new materials, have a look around your home to see what you could use instead. For example, you can cut cardboard shapes out of old boxes. You may have candies, rice paper, and writing icing for the fortune cookies in the cupboard, or you can buy them from a grocery store.

You can buy clay and drawing inks from a craft shop and other items such as alphabet transfers from a department store.

Getting started

Read the steps for the project first.

Gather together all the items you need.

Cover your work surface with newspaper.

Wear an apron, or change into old clothes.

A message for adults

All the projects in Friendship Crafts have been designed for children to make, but occasionally they will need you to help. Some of the projects do require the use of sharp utensils, such as scissors or needles. Please read through the instructions before your child starts work.

Making patterns

Follow these steps to make the patterns on pages 30 and 31. Using a pencil, trace the pattern onto tracing paper. To cut the pattern out of cardboard, turn the tracing over, and lay it onto the cardboard. Rub firmly over the pattern with a pencil. The shape will appear on the cardboard. Cut it out. To use a half pattern, trace the shape once, then flip over the tracing paper, and trace again to complete the whole shape. Or follow the instructions for the project.

When you have finished

Wash paintbrushes, and put everything away.

Put pens, pencils, paints, and glue in an old box or ice-cream container.

Keep scissors and any other sharp items in a safe place.

Stick needles and pins into a pincushion or a piece of scrap cloth.

BE SAFE

Look out for the safety boxes. They will appear whenever you need to ask an adult for help.

Ask an adult to help you use sharp scissors.

Linking lockets

This is a craft for you and your soul mate. The two pendants fit together to make a whole heart. They will remind you of your best friend even when you are apart.

YOU WILL NEED

air-drying clay
clay cutter
rolling pin
paint
varnish
paintbrush

ribbon or thick thread
star sequins
glue

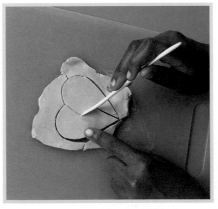

1 Roll out the clay to a thickness of ¼in (0.5cm). Cut out a heart shape, and then cut the heart in half with a zigzag line.

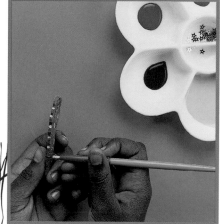

2 Make a hole at the top of each half using a pencil. Let the clay dry and harden. Paint both pieces pink.

3 When the pink paint is dry, paint dots and hearts in red and yellow onto the pendants. Go around each shape with a border of tiny dots in blue or yellow. We have glued on tiny star sequins, too.

4 Paint a stripy border in blue, red, and yellow around each piece. Let the paint dry. Varnish the heart pieces. Let them dry.

5 Thread ribbon or thick thread through the holes to make pendants. Give one half of the heart to a close friend.

Hand in hand

When a classmate leaves school, make a wall hanging of linking hands as a leaving gift. Each person in the class decorates a hand patch in his or her own distinctive way.

1 Cut squares of cardboard 6in x 6in (15cm x 15cm). Make one square for each of your friends to decorate. Make a hole in each corner using a hole punch.

YOU WILL NEED

scraps of fabric	ruler
felt in different colors	pencil
	glitter glue
wooden dowel	sequins
thin rope to hang up the hands	fabric paint
	fabric flower
cardboard	glue
hole punch	scissors
	thin wire

2 To decorate your square, cover the cardboard with fabric, and glue down the edges on the back of the square.

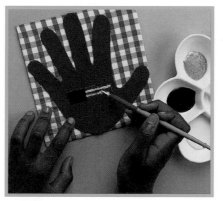

3 Draw around your hand onto a piece of felt, and cut out the shape.

4 Glue the hand onto the fabric square. Paint on a design using fabric paint, or glue on a fabric flower. We have glued on sequins and stuck on stickers to decorate some of the hands. Have fun, and sign your name on the back of the square with a goodbye message for your friend.

5 To make links to hold the squares together, wind wire around a piece of wooden dowel. Ask an adult to cut the wire spiral into circle sections.

Ask an adult to cut the wire links for you.

6 Poke the wire links through the corners of the fabric squares to connect them. Push a length of wooden dowel through the top row of wire links. You can hang up the hands by tying a length of thin rope to either end of the dowel.

9

Bubble book

Make this beautiful bubble print
paper to cover a book
full of friendship memories.
Glue in notes and cards from
your friends and photos of you all.

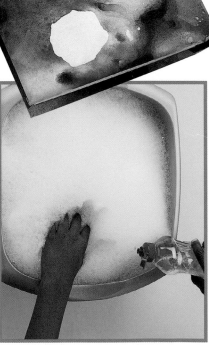

YOU WILL NEED

large tub

dishwashing
liquid

teaspoon

drawing inks

white paper

scrapbook

glue

scissors

1 Add some dishwashing liquid
to a big tub of water. Swish
it around with your hand to
make lots of bubbles.

10

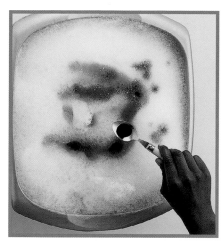

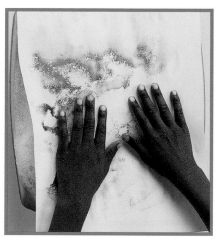

2 Trickle different colors of ink on top of the bubbles. Do this quickly, and get right on to the next step!

3 Lay a large sheet of white paper lightly on the bubbles. Take it off, and let it dry. You can print a few sheets from the same mixture.

4 To cover a large scrapbook, you may need to glue together two or more pieces.

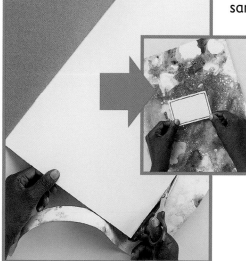

5 Glue the paper to the outside of a scrapbook. Trim the edges. Glue a paper label to the front so you can write your name on the book.

11

Fortune cookies

Write messages, dares, or
fortunes for all your friends,
and put them in these edible
packages. They're great fun
to hand out after a meal.

YOU WILL NEED

pencil	strawberry shoelaces
compass	candies
rice paper	
pinking shears	paper and pen
writing icing	hole punch

12

1 Draw circles onto rice paper using a compass. Our circles have a diameter of 4in (10cm). Cut out the circles inside the lines using pinking shears or scissors.

2 Fold a circle in half, and make four holes around the open edge using a hole punch. Write your message on a small piece of paper, and slip it inside the cookie.

3 Use a strawberry shoelace to lace the cookie closed. Tie together the two ends of the shoelace.

4 Stick candies with icing onto the cookies to make faces. Decorate the candy faces with writing icing.

Woven bracelet

Weaving a bracelet for a friend shows how much you care. To make this bracelet, weave ribbon through holes in a plastic frame. Take time designing the pattern before you begin.

1 Cut a strip 2in (5cm) wide from a large drink bottle. Draw around the piece of plastic onto graph paper so you can design your bracelet.

YOU WILL NEED

large plastic drink bottle	thin yellow ribbon
black marker pen	wide flowered ribbon
scissors	beads
thin red ribbon	felt-tip pens
thin blue ribbon	graph paper
	hole punch

2 Using colored felt-tip pens, draw a design onto the graph paper. Mark holes with black crosses, and plot which color ribbons you will thread through the holes. You can copy our design on page 30, or make up your own.

3 Lay the plastic strip over your design, and mark the crosses on the plastic, following the pattern. Punch holes where you have made crosses, using a hole punch.

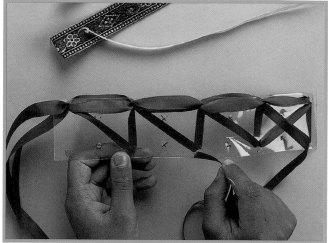

4 Begin by threading a thin blue ribbon along the top edge. Thread the ribbon in through the first hole and out through the next hole all the way along, then work back, filling in the gaps on each side. Now thread the red ribbon through, zigzagging across, and then zigzagging back to make crosses. Next, thread more of the blue ribbon along the bottom edge.

5 Thread thin yellow ribbon in stripes going down. Now pass a wide flowered ribbon under all the other ribbons around the middle of the bracelet. To finish your bracelet, tie the ribbon ends together, and tie beads onto the ends of one or two of the dangling ribbon strands.

Message decoder

Make a decoder for you and one for a friend. Turn the dial to set a code. Write a message using the letters you read off on the silver dial. Only your friend will be able to figure out the code!

1 Draw a circle with a diameter of 4in (10cm) on shiny red cardboard. Draw a smaller circle on silver cardboard and an even smaller circle on shiny red cardboard. Cut out the circles.

2 Lightly stick the silver circle on the center of the big red circle using masking tape. Draw a line through the center to divide the circles in half. Measure a little less than ½in (1cm) along the edge of the circle from this line, and make a mark. Draw a line from this mark through the center. Repeat to divide the circles into 26 equal segments.

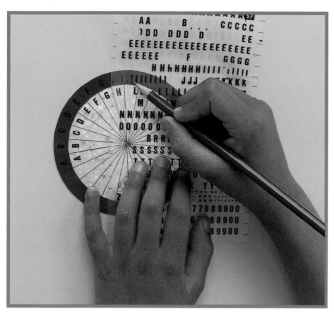

3 Use alphabet transfers or a pen to mark a letter of the alphabet in each segment of both circles as shown.

4 Decorate the small circle by gluing on sequin waste. Make a question mark with silver sequin stickers.

5 Stick silver sequin braid on the back of the big circle so it sticks out around the edge. Take off the masking tape and attach the circles together using a paper fastener.

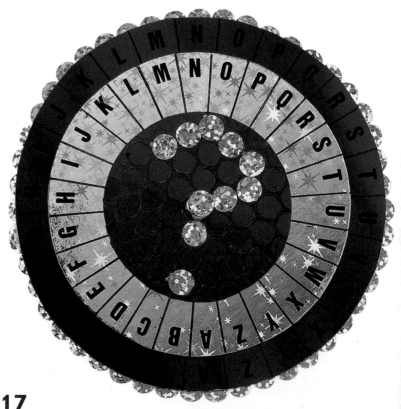

17

Tropical drink tray

Why not have a slumber party with a Hawaiian twist for your friends? Make a flowery tray to serve drinks. We have hollowed out melons to make little juice cups.

YOU WILL NEED

round tray	florist's wire
green fake fur as big as the tray	florist's tape
pink, orange, and yellow crêpe paper	pink, orange, and yellow acrylic paint
	paintbrush
pink, orange, and yellow long pipe cleaners	fabric glue
	scissors
	marker pen
gold glitter	

1 To make the flowers, roll up crêpe paper, and then cut a section 5in (12.5cm) long. Cut a section of orange and pink paper, too. Cut a point into one end of the crêpe sections as shown.

2 Unroll the crêpe paper, and cut the strips into five-petal pieces. You will need three of each color. Brush orange paint onto the center and edges of the yellow petals, and add dots, too. Paint the pink petals with yellow paint and the orange petals with pink paint.

18

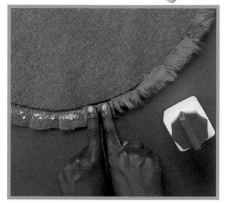

3 To make the flower stamens, bend two pieces of pipe cleaner in half. Twist florist's wire around them to keep them together. Choose pipe cleaners to match the color of the paint you used for each flower. Dip the ends of the stamens in fabric glue and then glitter.

4 Wrap the petals around the stamens and wire. Wind florist's tape around the bottom to keep them in place.

5 Draw around a round tray onto green fake fur fabric. Cut around the circle, leaving 1in (2.5cm) around the edge. Make snips in this border, and fold in each tab, gluing it down to make a neat edge.

6 Snip small holes around the edge of the fabric, and push the flowers through. Tape down the wire stems at the back. Place the grassy cover onto the tray, and pile on the midnight feast!

Green grub frame

Keep photos of your closest friends next to one another in this grub frame. It will look as if the grub has gobbled them up!

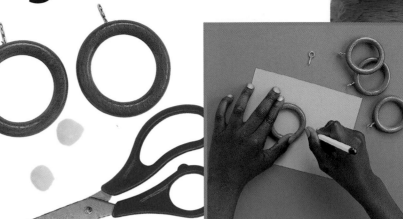

YOU WILL NEED

- four curtain rings
- green poster paint
- paintbrush
- green cardboard
- one pink and two yellow pipe cleaners
- two yellow pompoms
- pencil
- clear glue
- stiff white cardboard
- scissors
- black marker pen
- green fake fur

1 Unscrew the brass eyes from the curtain rings. Draw around a ring onto green cardboard. Draw and cut out four green circles in this way.

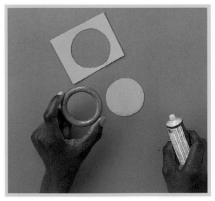

2 Glue the rings to the cardboard circles. Only glue halfway around, so there is a gap to slip in a photograph.

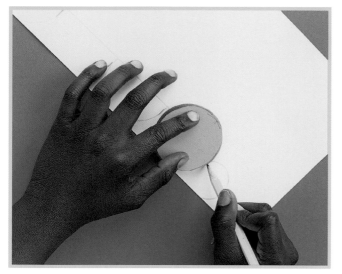

3 On a piece of white cardboard draw the grub's body and head. Draw around a curtain ring to get the shape right—the body is four circles in a row. Cut out the shape.

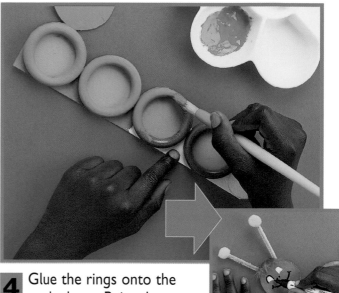

4 Glue the rings onto the grub shape. Paint the rings and the background green, but leave white spaces for the eyes. Draw on a face, and glue on pipe cleaners with pompoms for antennas. Glue on a tuft of fake fur hair, too.

6 Cut out pictures of your friends, and slip them into the ring frames.

5 Cut four pieces of yellow pipe cleaner, and bend them into V-shapes with feet. Put them over the grub between the rings, so that the grub stands up.

Pirate portrait

Have fun peering through the pirate portrait. Take photos of each other, and then try painting a different character's portrait.

1 Paint the cardboard white. This is a base coat to make the other colors show up well.

2 Trace the pirate's face on page 31. It is a half pattern so flip the tracing over, match the center lines, and trace again. Go over the pencil lines on one side. Now transfer the tracing onto the white cardboard following the instructions on page 5. Trace the hook, and transfer that onto the picture underneath the face.

3 Ask an adult to cut out the pirate's eye area and the mouth. She or he will find it easiest to use a craft knife.

Ask an adult to cut out the pirate's face using a craft knife.

4 Draw on a collar to finish the portrait. Now paint the pirate. Start with blocks of color, and then add shading in a different color. For example, add blue shading over the black beard.

5 Ask an adult to cut a frame for the portrait out of cardboard. Take the frame outside, and spray it gold. Stick it to the front of the portrait using double-sided tape.

Smile card

If you argue with a friend, give this sad/happy clown card to cheer them up. Write a message on the back to say why you miss them and want to make up.

YOU WILL NEED

white cardboard	poster paints
yellow cardboard 8½in x 11in (21.5cm x 28cm)	paintbrush
	glue
	black marker pen
felt-tip pens	shiny paper for the bow tie
scissors	
tracing paper	stick-on sequins
pencil	alphabet transfers
thin gift wrap ribbon	

PULL

1 Fold the yellow cardboard in half widthwise to find the center. Now unfold it, and fold the two edges into the center.

2 Trace the happy clown face on page 30. It is a half pattern, so flip over the tracing, and trace again for the whole face. Go over the pencil lines on one side, then transfer the tracing onto white cardboard following the instructions on page 5.

24

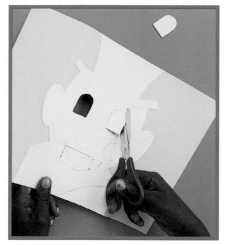

3 Cut out the clown, and glue him to the middle of the yellow cardboard—his ears will stick out over the edges. Cut out the eyes and a slit for the mouth as shown on the pattern.

4 Trace the sad mouth pattern on page 30, and transfer the tracing onto white cardboard. Next, cut out the shape and then the mouth slit as shown on the pattern.

5 Paint the happy clown's lips red, and paint on pink cheeks and a stripy outfit. Paint the sad mouth red, and paint green strips above the eyes. Let the paint dry. Go over the eyebrows and lips with a pen.

6 Fold back the yellow card edges, and tape them at the back. Slip the sad mouth inside so that the tab pokes out. Mark "Pull" on the top of the tab with transfers. Decorate the hat with shiny paper and stickers, and fold shiny paper in a concertina to make a bow tie. Curl gift-wrap ribbon by running closed scissors along each strip. Glue it on to make hair.

25

Sunshine badge

Show the sunbeams in your life that you care! Make fun badges with different shapes and messages as surprises for your friends on special days.

YOU WILL NEED

yellow craft foam	thin scrap cardboard
compass and pencil	scissors
gold glitter pen	orange and gold paint
glue	paintbrush
brooch back	

1 Draw a circle onto yellow craft foam using a compass. Our circle has a diameter of 2½in (6cm). Draw two small flame shapes on scrap cardboard. Cut them out, and draw around them to give the sun a flaming edge.

4 Decorate the center of the sun with gold glitter. You can write on a message with a gold glitter pen. We have written, "You are my" (sunshine)!

2 Draw a second circle onto craft foam, and cut it out. Cut out the flaming sun, too. Glue the circle on top of the sun.

3 Paint orange and gold streaks onto the sun's flames.

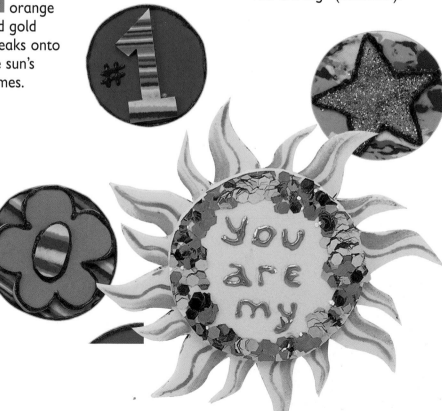

5 Glue a brooch back to the back of the badge.

27

Claddagh box

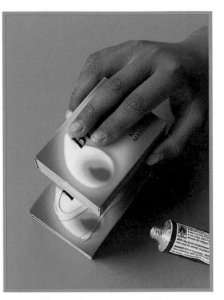

The claddagh is an Irish symbol of love and friendship. It shows two hands clasping a heart. Decorate this tiny chest of drawers with purple velvet and a golden claddagh to make a dainty secrets box.

YOU WILL NEED

tracing paper	gold sequins shaped like leaves
three medium-size matchboxes	purple velvety fabric
glue	gold fabric pen
purple poster paint	plastic jewels
paintbrush	felt-tip pen
purple craft foam	tiny beads

1 Glue three matchboxes together, one on top of the other.

2 Paint the individual drawers purple and the front edges of the chest purple, too.

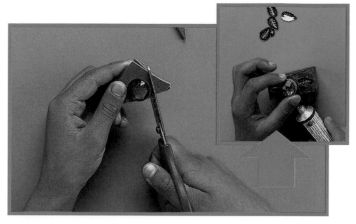

3 Cover the chest of drawers with purple velvety fabric. Glue a rectangle of fabric to one end of each drawer as well.

4 Use three plastic jewels to make drawer handles. Glue each jewel onto craft foam, and cut out the foam around the jewel. Glue each handle to the front of a drawer. Glue a leaf sequin on either side.

5 Copy the claddagh design on page 31 onto the side of the drawers. Go over the design using a gold fabric pen. Glue on tiny beads at the crown tips and a yellow plastic jewel on the heart.

Patterns

Here are the patterns you will need to make some of the projects. To find out how to make a pattern, follow the instructions in the "Making patterns" box on page 5. Some of the patterns are half patterns. There are instructions to help you use the half patterns in the steps for the projects. The bracelet and claddagh designs are for you to copy. You don't need to copy them exactly; they are to help you with your own designs.

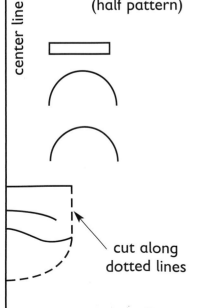

center line

Smile card
page 24

(half pattern)

cut along
dotted lines

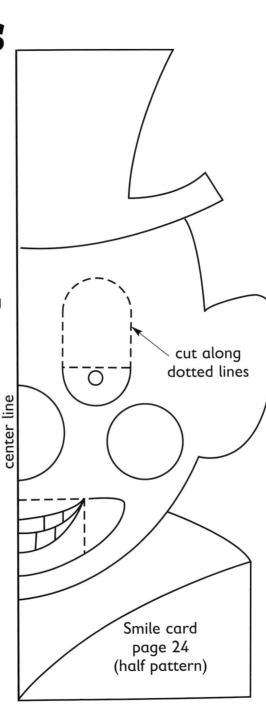

center line

cut along
dotted lines

Smile card
page 24
(half pattern)

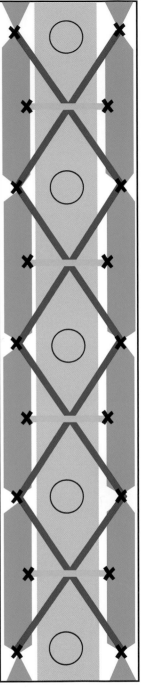

Woven bracelet
page 14

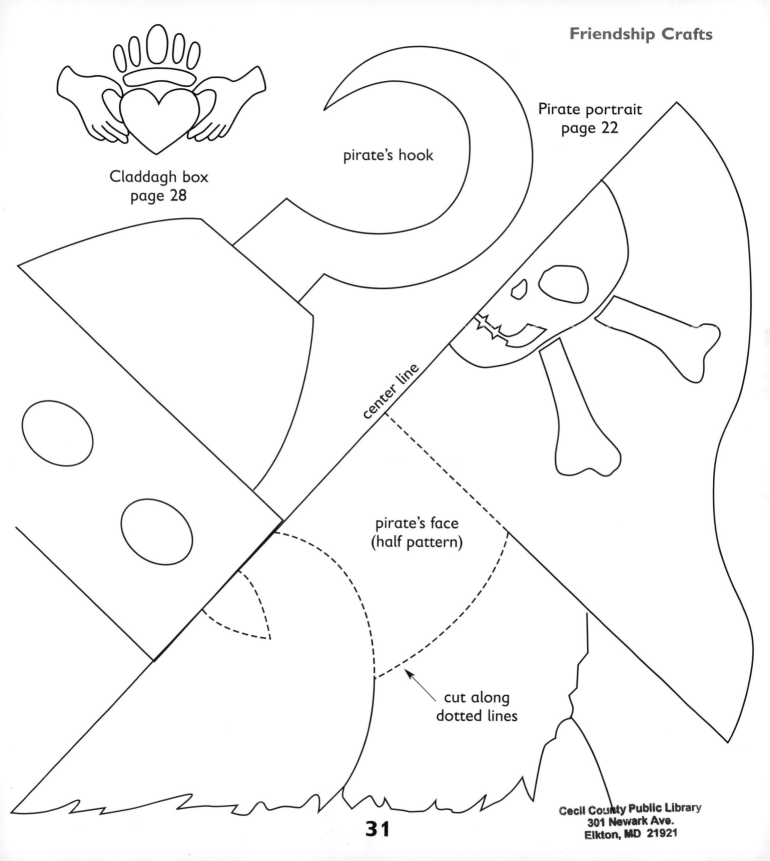

Claddagh box
page 28

pirate's hook

Pirate portrait
page 22

center line

pirate's face
(half pattern)

cut along
dotted lines

Glossary

acrylic paint a paint, used especially for painting pictures, that is made with a manufactured acid

brooch a piece of jewelry that is fastened to clothing by a pin

claddagh a design of Irish origin consisting of two hands clasping a heart, with a crown positioned above them

grizzly describing hair, especially on men, that is streaked with gray

grub a wormlike, immature form of some insects

pendant a piece of jewelry that hangs from a necklace

pinking shears scissors with blades that cut zigzag edges in cloth

portrait a painting, photograph, or drawing of a person or people

stamen an organ of a flower, usually consisting of a stalk and the part of the flower that produces pollen

transfer an image on a piece of paper or film that is designed to be lifted off by heat or pressure and applied to another surface

varnish a substance that gives an object a protective gloss, or the act of applying this substance

Index